50 American Night Recipes for Home

By: Kelly Johnson

Table of Contents

- Classic Cheeseburger
- BBQ Ribs
- Macaroni and Cheese
- Chicken Pot Pie
- New York Style Pizza
- Buffalo Wings
- Southern Fried Chicken
- Texas Chili
- Philly Cheesesteak
- Lobster Mac and Cheese
- Chicago Deep Dish Pizza
- Shrimp and Grits
- Cajun Jambalaya
- Hawaiian Pizza
- California Cobb Salad
- Texas BBQ Brisket
- Maryland Crab Cakes
- Boston Clam Chowder
- Philly Cheesesteak Sandwich
- Mississippi Mud Pie
- New England Clam Bake
- Kansas City BBQ Ribs
- Wisconsin Beer Brats
- Tex-Mex Enchiladas
- Florida Key Lime Pie
- Memphis BBQ Pulled Pork
- New Orleans Gumbo
- Colorado Green Chili
- Texas Sheet Cake
- Chicago Hot Dog
- New York Cheesecake
- California Fish Tacos
- Maine Lobster Roll
- Hawaiian Huli Huli Chicken
- Southern Shrimp and Grits

- Philadelphia Soft Pretzels
- Louisiana Crawfish Boil
- San Francisco Cioppino
- Texas Chili Dogs
- Kentucky Hot Brown
- Vermont Maple Syrup Pancakes
- Tennessee Hot Chicken
- Detroit-Style Coney Dog
- Hawaiian Loco Moco
- Texas Chicken Fried Steak
- California Club Sandwich
- New York Reuben Sandwich
- Maryland Crab Soup
- Chicago Italian Beef Sandwich
- Florida Key Lime Pie

Classic Cheeseburger

Ingredients:

- 1 pound ground beef (80/20 lean to fat ratio)
- Salt and pepper, to taste
- 4 hamburger buns
- 4 slices of cheese (American, cheddar, or your choice)
- Optional toppings: lettuce, tomato, onion, pickles, ketchup, mustard, mayonnaise

Instructions:

1. Preheat your grill or skillet to medium-high heat.
2. Divide the ground beef into four equal portions and shape them into patties. Make a slight indentation in the center of each patty with your thumb to prevent it from bulging during cooking. Season both sides of the patties generously with salt and pepper.
3. Place the patties on the grill or skillet and cook for about 4-5 minutes on each side, or until they reach your desired level of doneness. If adding cheese, place a slice on each patty during the last minute of cooking and allow it to melt.
4. While the patties are cooking, lightly toast the hamburger buns on the grill or skillet.
5. Assemble the burgers by placing the cooked patties on the bottom half of each bun. Add your desired toppings, such as lettuce, tomato, onion, pickles, ketchup, mustard, and mayonnaise. Top with the other half of the bun.
6. Serve immediately and enjoy your classic cheeseburgers!

BBQ Ribs

Ingredients:

- 2 racks of pork ribs (baby back or spare ribs)
- 2 cups BBQ sauce (store-bought or homemade)
- 2 tablespoons brown sugar
- 1 tablespoon paprika
- 1 tablespoon garlic powder
- 1 tablespoon onion powder
- 1 tablespoon salt
- 1 teaspoon black pepper
- Optional: additional BBQ rub or seasoning blend

Instructions:

1. Preheat your oven to 275°F (135°C).
2. Remove the membrane from the back of the ribs if it's still attached. Use a knife to loosen the edge of the membrane, then grip it with a paper towel and peel it off.
3. In a small bowl, mix together the brown sugar, paprika, garlic powder, onion powder, salt, and black pepper to make a dry rub.
4. Rub the dry rub all over the ribs, covering them evenly. You can also use any additional BBQ rub or seasoning blend you prefer.
5. Wrap each rack of ribs tightly in aluminum foil, creating a sealed packet.
6. Place the foil-wrapped ribs on a baking sheet and bake in the preheated oven for 2.5 to 3 hours, or until the meat is tender and begins to pull away from the bones.
7. Carefully remove the foil from the ribs and drain off any excess liquid.
8. Increase the oven temperature to 375°F (190°C).
9. Brush the BBQ sauce generously over the ribs, coating them evenly.
10. Return the ribs to the oven, uncovered, and bake for an additional 15-20 minutes, or until the sauce is caramelized and sticky.
11. Remove the ribs from the oven and let them rest for a few minutes before slicing.
12. Serve the BBQ ribs with any extra BBQ sauce on the side and enjoy!

Macaroni and Cheese

Ingredients:

- 8 oz (about 2 cups) elbow macaroni
- 4 tbsp unsalted butter
- 1/4 cup all-purpose flour
- 2 cups whole milk
- 2 cups shredded sharp cheddar cheese
- 1 cup shredded mozzarella cheese
- 1/2 cup grated Parmesan cheese
- 1/2 tsp salt
- 1/4 tsp black pepper
- 1/4 tsp paprika (optional, for garnish)
- 1/4 cup breadcrumbs (optional, for topping)

Instructions:

1. Preheat your oven to 350°F (175°C). Grease a 9x13-inch baking dish and set aside.
2. Cook the elbow macaroni according to the package instructions until al dente. Drain and set aside.
3. In a large saucepan, melt the butter over medium heat. Once melted, add the flour and whisk continuously for about 1-2 minutes to make a roux.
4. Gradually pour in the milk while whisking constantly to avoid lumps. Cook the mixture until it thickens and becomes smooth, about 3-5 minutes.
5. Reduce the heat to low and stir in the shredded cheddar, mozzarella, and Parmesan cheese until melted and smooth.
6. Season the cheese sauce with salt and black pepper to taste.
7. Add the cooked macaroni to the cheese sauce and stir until well combined.
8. Pour the macaroni and cheese mixture into the prepared baking dish, spreading it out evenly.
9. If desired, sprinkle paprika over the top for color and sprinkle breadcrumbs for a crispy topping.
10. Bake in the preheated oven for 25-30 minutes, or until the top is golden brown and bubbly.
11. Remove from the oven and let it cool for a few minutes before serving.
12. Serve hot and enjoy your delicious homemade macaroni and cheese!

Feel free to customize this recipe by adding cooked bacon, diced ham, diced tomatoes, or green onions for extra flavor.

Chicken Pot Pie

Ingredients:

For the Pie Crust:

- 2 1/2 cups all-purpose flour
- 1 teaspoon salt
- 1 cup unsalted butter, cold and cubed
- 6-8 tablespoons ice water

For the Filling:

- 2 tablespoons unsalted butter
- 1 small onion, chopped
- 2 carrots, diced
- 2 celery stalks, diced
- 2 cloves garlic, minced
- 1/4 cup all-purpose flour
- 2 cups chicken broth
- 1 cup whole milk
- 2 cups cooked chicken, diced or shredded
- 1 cup frozen peas
- 1 teaspoon dried thyme
- Salt and pepper, to taste

Instructions:

1. Start by making the pie crust. In a large bowl, whisk together the flour and salt. Add the cubed butter and use a pastry cutter or fork to cut it into the flour mixture until it resembles coarse crumbs.
2. Gradually add the ice water, 1 tablespoon at a time, mixing with a fork until the dough just comes together. Be careful not to overmix. Divide the dough into two equal portions, shape each into a disk, wrap in plastic wrap, and refrigerate for at least 30 minutes.
3. Preheat the oven to 375°F (190°C).
4. In a large skillet, melt the butter over medium heat. Add the chopped onion, carrots, and celery, and cook until softened, about 5-7 minutes. Add the minced garlic and cook for an additional minute.

5. Sprinkle the flour over the vegetables and stir to combine. Cook for 1-2 minutes to remove the raw flour taste.
6. Gradually pour in the chicken broth and milk, stirring constantly until the mixture thickens.
7. Add the cooked chicken, frozen peas, dried thyme, salt, and pepper to the skillet. Stir until everything is well combined and heated through. Remove from heat and set aside.
8. Roll out one of the chilled pie crust disks on a lightly floured surface to fit the bottom of a 9-inch pie dish. Transfer the crust to the pie dish and gently press it into the bottom and sides.
9. Pour the chicken filling into the prepared pie crust.
10. Roll out the second pie crust disk and place it over the filling. Trim any excess dough and crimp the edges to seal. Cut a few slits in the top crust to allow steam to escape.
11. Optional: Brush the top crust with beaten egg for a shiny finish.
12. Place the pie on a baking sheet to catch any drips and bake in the preheated oven for 45-50 minutes, or until the crust is golden brown and the filling is bubbly.
13. Remove from the oven and let it cool for a few minutes before serving.
14. Slice and serve your delicious homemade chicken pot pie, and enjoy the comforting flavors!

New York Style Pizza

Ingredients:

For the Pizza Dough:

- 3 1/2 cups bread flour
- 1 teaspoon sugar
- 1 envelope (2 1/4 teaspoons) active dry yeast
- 2 teaspoons salt
- 1 1/2 cups warm water (110°F/45°C)
- 2 tablespoons olive oil

For the Pizza Sauce:

- 1 can (28 ounces) crushed tomatoes
- 2 cloves garlic, minced
- 1 teaspoon dried oregano
- 1 teaspoon dried basil
- Salt and pepper, to taste

For the Toppings:

- 2 cups shredded mozzarella cheese
- Optional: additional toppings such as pepperoni, sausage, mushrooms, bell peppers, onions, etc.

Instructions:

1. To make the pizza dough, in a large mixing bowl, combine the bread flour, sugar, yeast, and salt. Gradually add the warm water and olive oil, stirring until a dough forms.
2. Turn the dough out onto a lightly floured surface and knead for about 5-7 minutes, or until smooth and elastic. Shape the dough into a ball.
3. Place the dough ball in a greased bowl, cover with plastic wrap or a kitchen towel, and let it rise in a warm place for about 1 to 1 1/2 hours, or until doubled in size.

4. While the dough is rising, make the pizza sauce. In a saucepan, combine the crushed tomatoes, minced garlic, dried oregano, and dried basil. Season with salt and pepper to taste. Simmer the sauce over low heat for about 20-30 minutes, stirring occasionally, until thickened.
5. Preheat your oven to 475°F (245°C) and place a pizza stone or inverted baking sheet in the oven to preheat as well.
6. Once the dough has risen, punch it down and divide it into two equal portions. Roll out each portion of dough on a lightly floured surface into a circle about 12 inches in diameter.
7. Transfer the rolled-out dough to a piece of parchment paper dusted with cornmeal to prevent sticking.
8. Spread a thin layer of pizza sauce over the dough, leaving a small border around the edges. Sprinkle shredded mozzarella cheese evenly over the sauce, and add any additional toppings as desired.
9. Carefully transfer the pizza (on the parchment paper) to the preheated pizza stone or baking sheet in the oven.
10. Bake the pizza for about 12-15 minutes, or until the crust is golden brown and the cheese is melted and bubbly.
11. Remove the pizza from the oven and let it cool for a few minutes before slicing.
12. Serve hot and enjoy your homemade New York-style pizza!

Feel free to customize your pizza with your favorite toppings and experiment with different combinations to suit your taste preferences.

Buffalo Wings

Ingredients:

For the Wings:

- 2 pounds chicken wings, split into drumettes and flats
- 1 tablespoon vegetable oil
- Salt and pepper, to taste

For the Sauce:

- 1/2 cup hot sauce (such as Frank's RedHot)
- 1/4 cup unsalted butter
- 1 tablespoon white vinegar
- 1/2 teaspoon Worcestershire sauce
- 1/4 teaspoon garlic powder
- 1/4 teaspoon cayenne pepper (optional, for extra heat)

For Serving:

- Celery sticks
- Carrot sticks
- Ranch or blue cheese dressing

Instructions:

1. Preheat your oven to 400°F (200°C). Line a baking sheet with aluminum foil and place a wire rack on top.
2. In a large bowl, toss the chicken wings with vegetable oil, salt, and pepper until evenly coated.
3. Arrange the wings in a single layer on the wire rack on the prepared baking sheet. Bake in the preheated oven for 45-50 minutes, or until the wings are golden brown and crispy, flipping halfway through cooking.
4. While the wings are baking, prepare the sauce. In a small saucepan, combine the hot sauce, unsalted butter, white vinegar, Worcestershire sauce, garlic powder, and cayenne pepper (if using). Heat over medium heat, stirring occasionally, until the butter is melted and the sauce is heated through. Remove from heat and set aside.

5. Once the wings are cooked, transfer them to a large bowl. Pour the Buffalo sauce over the wings and toss until evenly coated.
6. Serve the Buffalo wings hot with celery sticks, carrot sticks, and your choice of ranch or blue cheese dressing for dipping.
7. Enjoy your homemade Buffalo wings as a delicious appetizer or main dish for game day or any occasion!

Feel free to adjust the amount of hot sauce and cayenne pepper in the sauce according to your desired level of spiciness. You can also grill or fry the wings instead of baking them if preferred.

Southern Fried Chicken

Ingredients:

- 2 lbs chicken pieces (such as thighs, drumsticks, or breasts), skin-on
- 2 cups buttermilk
- 2 cups all-purpose flour
- 1 tablespoon salt
- 1 tablespoon black pepper
- 1 tablespoon paprika
- 1 teaspoon garlic powder
- 1 teaspoon onion powder
- Vegetable oil, for frying

Instructions:

1. Place the chicken pieces in a large bowl and pour the buttermilk over them. Make sure the chicken is fully submerged. Cover the bowl and refrigerate for at least 4 hours or overnight to marinate.
2. In a shallow dish or pie plate, combine the flour, salt, pepper, paprika, garlic powder, and onion powder. Mix well to combine.
3. Remove the chicken from the buttermilk marinade, allowing any excess to drip off.
4. Dredge each chicken piece in the seasoned flour mixture, coating it thoroughly. Shake off any excess flour.
5. Heat about 1 inch of vegetable oil in a large skillet or Dutch oven over medium-high heat until it reaches 350°F (175°C) on a deep-fry thermometer.
6. Carefully place the chicken pieces in the hot oil, skin-side down, making sure not to overcrowd the pan. Fry the chicken in batches if necessary.
7. Fry the chicken for about 6-8 minutes per side, or until golden brown and crispy and the internal temperature reaches 165°F (75°C) for dark meat or 160°F (70°C) for white meat.
8. Once cooked, remove the chicken from the oil and transfer it to a wire rack set over a baking sheet to drain excess oil. Allow the chicken to rest for a few minutes before serving.
9. Serve the Southern fried chicken hot, accompanied by your favorite sides such as mashed potatoes, coleslaw, biscuits, or gravy.
10. Enjoy your homemade Southern fried chicken, with its crispy golden crust and juicy tender meat!

Texas Chili

Ingredients:

- 2 pounds beef chuck, cut into 1/2-inch cubes
- 2 tablespoons vegetable oil
- 1 large onion, chopped
- 4 cloves garlic, minced
- 2 tablespoons chili powder
- 1 tablespoon ground cumin
- 1 tablespoon paprika
- 1 teaspoon dried oregano
- 1 teaspoon cayenne pepper (adjust to taste)
- 1 teaspoon salt (adjust to taste)
- 1/2 teaspoon black pepper
- 1 can (14.5 ounces) diced tomatoes
- 1 can (6 ounces) tomato paste
- 2 cups beef broth
- 1 can (15 ounces) kidney beans, drained and rinsed (optional)
- Optional toppings: shredded cheese, chopped onions, sour cream, cilantro, jalapeños

Instructions:

1. In a large pot or Dutch oven, heat the vegetable oil over medium-high heat. Add the cubed beef and cook until browned on all sides, about 5-7 minutes. Remove the beef from the pot and set aside.
2. In the same pot, add the chopped onion and cook until softened, about 5 minutes. Add the minced garlic and cook for an additional minute.
3. Return the browned beef to the pot. Add the chili powder, ground cumin, paprika, dried oregano, cayenne pepper, salt, and black pepper. Stir well to coat the beef and onions with the spices.
4. Add the diced tomatoes (with their juices), tomato paste, and beef broth to the pot. Stir to combine.
5. Bring the chili to a boil, then reduce the heat to low. Cover and simmer for about 1 1/2 to 2 hours, stirring occasionally, until the beef is tender and the flavors have melded together.
6. If using kidney beans, add them to the chili during the last 30 minutes of cooking. This step is optional and traditional Texas chili does not typically include beans.

7. Taste the chili and adjust the seasoning with additional salt and pepper if needed.
8. Serve the Texas chili hot, garnished with your favorite toppings such as shredded cheese, chopped onions, sour cream, cilantro, or jalapeños.
9. Enjoy your homemade Texas-style chili, packed with bold flavors and hearty chunks of beef!

Philly Cheesesteak

Ingredients:

- 1 pound ribeye steak, thinly sliced
- 2 tablespoons vegetable oil, divided
- 1 large onion, thinly sliced
- 1 large green bell pepper, thinly sliced
- Salt and pepper, to taste
- 4 hoagie rolls, split lengthwise
- 8 slices provolone cheese

Instructions:

1. Heat 1 tablespoon of vegetable oil in a large skillet over medium-high heat. Add the thinly sliced ribeye steak to the skillet and cook, stirring occasionally, until browned and cooked through, about 3-5 minutes. Season with salt and pepper to taste. Remove the steak from the skillet and set aside.
2. In the same skillet, add the remaining tablespoon of vegetable oil. Add the thinly sliced onion and green bell pepper to the skillet and cook, stirring occasionally, until softened and lightly caramelized, about 5-7 minutes. Season with salt and pepper to taste.
3. Return the cooked steak to the skillet with the onions and peppers, and toss everything together until well combined. Cook for an additional 1-2 minutes to heat through.
4. Preheat your oven's broiler.
5. Open the hoagie rolls and place them cut-side up on a baking sheet. Divide the steak, onion, and pepper mixture evenly among the rolls, spreading it out in an even layer.
6. Top each sandwich with 2 slices of provolone cheese.
7. Place the baking sheet under the broiler and broil for 1-2 minutes, or until the cheese is melted and bubbly and the edges of the rolls are toasted.
8. Remove the Philly cheesesteak sandwiches from the oven and serve immediately.
9. Enjoy your homemade Philly cheesesteaks, packed with tender ribeye steak, sautéed onions and peppers, and gooey melted provolone cheese, all piled high on a toasted hoagie roll!

Lobster Mac and Cheese

Ingredients:

- 8 oz macaroni pasta
- 2 lobster tails, cooked and chopped
- 4 tablespoons unsalted butter
- 1/4 cup all-purpose flour
- 2 cups whole milk
- 1 cup heavy cream
- 2 cups shredded sharp cheddar cheese
- 1 cup shredded Gruyere cheese
- 1/2 cup grated Parmesan cheese
- 1/4 teaspoon cayenne pepper (optional)
- Salt and pepper, to taste
- 1/2 cup panko breadcrumbs
- 2 tablespoons chopped fresh parsley

Instructions:

1. Preheat your oven to 375°F (190°C). Grease a 9x13-inch baking dish and set aside.
2. Cook the macaroni pasta according to the package instructions until al dente. Drain and set aside.
3. In a large saucepan, melt the butter over medium heat. Once melted, add the flour and whisk continuously for about 1-2 minutes to make a roux.
4. Gradually pour in the milk and heavy cream, whisking constantly to avoid lumps. Cook the mixture until it thickens and becomes smooth, about 5-7 minutes.
5. Reduce the heat to low and add the shredded cheddar, Gruyere, and Parmesan cheese to the saucepan. Stir until the cheese is melted and the sauce is smooth. Season with cayenne pepper (if using), salt, and pepper to taste.
6. Add the cooked macaroni pasta and chopped lobster tails to the cheese sauce, stirring until everything is well coated.
7. Transfer the lobster mac and cheese mixture to the prepared baking dish, spreading it out evenly.
8. In a small bowl, mix together the panko breadcrumbs and chopped parsley. Sprinkle the breadcrumb mixture evenly over the top of the mac and cheese.

9. Bake in the preheated oven for 25-30 minutes, or until the top is golden brown and the cheese is bubbly.
10. Remove from the oven and let it cool for a few minutes before serving.
11. Serve your delicious lobster mac and cheese hot as a main dish or side, and enjoy the creamy, cheesy goodness with tender chunks of lobster!

Chicago Deep Dish Pizza

Ingredients:

For the Dough:

- 3 1/4 cups all-purpose flour
- 1/2 cup cornmeal
- 1 tablespoon sugar
- 1 teaspoon salt
- 1 packet (2 1/4 teaspoons) active dry yeast
- 1 1/4 cups warm water (110°F/45°C)
- 1/4 cup unsalted butter, melted
- 2 tablespoons olive oil

For the Pizza:

- 1 pound Italian sausage, cooked and crumbled (optional)
- 2 cups shredded mozzarella cheese
- 1 cup grated Parmesan cheese
- 1 cup marinara sauce
- 1 cup sliced mushrooms
- 1/2 cup sliced green bell peppers
- 1/2 cup sliced onions
- Additional toppings of your choice (pepperoni, olives, etc.)

Instructions:

1. In a large mixing bowl, combine the all-purpose flour, cornmeal, sugar, salt, and active dry yeast. Mix well.
2. Add the warm water and melted butter to the dry ingredients. Stir until a dough forms.
3. Turn the dough out onto a lightly floured surface and knead for about 5 minutes, or until smooth and elastic.
4. Grease a deep dish pizza pan (about 9-10 inches in diameter) with olive oil. Press the dough evenly into the bottom and up the sides of the pan, forming a crust.
5. Preheat your oven to 425°F (220°C).

6. Layer the cooked Italian sausage (if using) on the bottom of the pizza crust.
7. Sprinkle half of the shredded mozzarella cheese over the sausage layer.
8. Spread the marinara sauce over the cheese layer.
9. Add the sliced mushrooms, green bell peppers, onions, and any other toppings of your choice.
10. Sprinkle the remaining shredded mozzarella cheese and grated Parmesan cheese over the top of the pizza.
11. Cover the pizza loosely with aluminum foil and bake in the preheated oven for 20 minutes.
12. Remove the foil and continue baking for an additional 15-20 minutes, or until the crust is golden brown and the cheese is melted and bubbly.
13. Remove the pizza from the oven and let it cool in the pan for a few minutes before slicing and serving.
14. Enjoy your homemade Chicago-style deep dish pizza, with its thick, buttery crust and layers of savory toppings!

Shrimp and Grits

Ingredients:

For the Shrimp:

- 1 pound large shrimp, peeled and deveined
- 1 tablespoon Cajun seasoning (or a mix of paprika, garlic powder, onion powder, cayenne pepper, salt, and pepper)
- 2 tablespoons unsalted butter
- 2 cloves garlic, minced
- 2 tablespoons lemon juice
- Salt and pepper, to taste
- Chopped fresh parsley, for garnish

For the Grits:

- 1 cup stone-ground grits
- 4 cups water or chicken broth
- 1/2 cup heavy cream
- 2 tablespoons unsalted butter
- Salt and pepper, to taste

Instructions:

1. In a medium saucepan, bring the water or chicken broth to a boil. Gradually whisk in the stone-ground grits, reduce the heat to low, and cover. Cook the grits for 20-25 minutes, stirring occasionally, until thickened and creamy.
2. Stir in the heavy cream and unsalted butter until well combined. Season the grits with salt and pepper to taste. Keep warm while you prepare the shrimp.
3. In a large bowl, toss the peeled and deveined shrimp with Cajun seasoning until evenly coated.
4. Heat a large skillet over medium-high heat. Add the unsalted butter and minced garlic to the skillet and cook until fragrant, about 1 minute.
5. Add the seasoned shrimp to the skillet in a single layer. Cook for 2-3 minutes on each side, or until pink and cooked through. Be careful not to overcook the shrimp.

6. Once the shrimp are cooked, squeeze lemon juice over them and season with salt and pepper to taste.
7. To serve, spoon the creamy grits into bowls and top with the cooked shrimp. Garnish with chopped fresh parsley for added flavor and color.
8. Enjoy your homemade shrimp and grits as a comforting and flavorful Southern-inspired dish!

Feel free to customize this recipe by adding crispy bacon or diced Andouille sausage to the grits for extra flavor. You can also add diced tomatoes, green onions, or bell peppers to the shrimp for added texture and flavor.

Cajun Jambalaya

Ingredients:

- 1 pound boneless, skinless chicken thighs, cut into bite-sized pieces
- 1 pound Andouille sausage, sliced
- 1 large onion, diced
- 1 bell pepper, diced
- 2 stalks celery, diced
- 3 cloves garlic, minced
- 1 can (14.5 ounces) diced tomatoes
- 1 cup long-grain white rice
- 2 cups chicken broth
- 2 teaspoons Cajun seasoning
- 1 teaspoon paprika
- 1/2 teaspoon dried thyme
- 1/2 teaspoon dried oregano
- Salt and pepper, to taste
- 2 green onions, thinly sliced (for garnish)
- Chopped fresh parsley (for garnish)

Instructions:

1. Heat a large skillet or Dutch oven over medium-high heat. Add the sliced Andouille sausage and cook until browned, about 4-5 minutes. Remove the sausage from the skillet and set aside.
2. In the same skillet, add the diced chicken thighs. Cook until browned on all sides and cooked through, about 5-6 minutes. Remove the chicken from the skillet and set aside with the cooked sausage.
3. In the same skillet, add the diced onion, bell pepper, and celery. Cook until softened, about 5-7 minutes.
4. Add the minced garlic to the skillet and cook for an additional 1-2 minutes, until fragrant.
5. Stir in the diced tomatoes (with their juices), rice, chicken broth, Cajun seasoning, paprika, dried thyme, dried oregano, salt, and pepper.
6. Return the cooked sausage and chicken to the skillet. Stir everything together until well combined.

7. Bring the mixture to a boil, then reduce the heat to low. Cover and simmer for 20-25 minutes, or until the rice is cooked and the liquid is absorbed.
8. Remove the skillet from the heat and let it sit, covered, for 5 minutes.
9. Fluff the jambalaya with a fork and garnish with thinly sliced green onions and chopped fresh parsley before serving.
10. Serve your delicious Cajun jambalaya hot, and enjoy the bold flavors of this classic Southern dish!

Feel free to customize this recipe by adding shrimp, crabmeat, or other seafood along with the chicken and sausage for a seafood jambalaya. Adjust the Cajun seasoning to your preferred level of spiciness.

Hawaiian Pizza

Ingredients:

- 1 pre-made pizza dough (or homemade if you prefer)
- 1/2 cup pizza sauce
- 1 1/2 cups shredded mozzarella cheese
- 1 cup diced pineapple (fresh or canned)
- 1/2 cup diced ham or Canadian bacon
- Olive oil (for brushing the crust, optional)
- Red pepper flakes (optional, for added spice)

Instructions:

1. Preheat your oven to the temperature specified on your pizza dough package or to 425°F (220°C) if you're using homemade dough.
2. Roll out the pizza dough on a lightly floured surface to your desired thickness. Transfer the rolled-out dough to a pizza pan or baking sheet lined with parchment paper.
3. Spread the pizza sauce evenly over the dough, leaving a small border around the edges for the crust.
4. Sprinkle the shredded mozzarella cheese over the sauce, covering the entire surface of the pizza.
5. Distribute the diced pineapple and diced ham or Canadian bacon evenly over the cheese.
6. If desired, sprinkle a pinch of red pepper flakes over the toppings for added spice.
7. Optionally, brush the edges of the crust with olive oil for a golden finish.
8. Place the pizza in the preheated oven and bake for 12-15 minutes, or until the crust is golden brown and the cheese is bubbly and melted.
9. Once baked, remove the pizza from the oven and let it cool for a few minutes before slicing.
10. Slice the pizza into wedges and serve hot. Enjoy your homemade Hawaiian pizza!

Feel free to customize the recipe according to your preferences by adding other toppings like bacon, bell peppers, onions, or even jalapeños for an extra kick.

California Cobb Salad

Ingredients:

- 1 pound boneless, skinless chicken thighs, cut into bite-sized pieces
- 1 pound Andouille sausage, sliced
- 1 large onion, diced
- 1 bell pepper, diced
- 2 stalks celery, diced
- 3 cloves garlic, minced
- 1 can (14.5 ounces) diced tomatoes
- 1 cup long-grain white rice
- 2 cups chicken broth
- 2 teaspoons Cajun seasoning
- 1 teaspoon paprika
- 1/2 teaspoon dried thyme
- 1/2 teaspoon dried oregano
- Salt and pepper, to taste
- 2 green onions, thinly sliced (for garnish)
- Chopped fresh parsley (for garnish)

Instructions:

1. Heat a large skillet or Dutch oven over medium-high heat. Add the sliced Andouille sausage and cook until browned, about 4-5 minutes. Remove the sausage from the skillet and set aside.
2. In the same skillet, add the diced chicken thighs. Cook until browned on all sides and cooked through, about 5-6 minutes. Remove the chicken from the skillet and set aside with the cooked sausage.
3. In the same skillet, add the diced onion, bell pepper, and celery. Cook until softened, about 5-7 minutes.
4. Add the minced garlic to the skillet and cook for an additional 1-2 minutes, until fragrant.
5. Stir in the diced tomatoes (with their juices), rice, chicken broth, Cajun seasoning, paprika, dried thyme, dried oregano, salt, and pepper.
6. Return the cooked sausage and chicken to the skillet. Stir everything together until well combined.

7. Bring the mixture to a boil, then reduce the heat to low. Cover and simmer for 20-25 minutes, or until the rice is cooked and the liquid is absorbed.
8. Remove the skillet from the heat and let it sit, covered, for 5 minutes.
9. Fluff the jambalaya with a fork and garnish with thinly sliced green onions and chopped fresh parsley before serving.
10. Serve your delicious Cajun jambalaya hot, and enjoy the bold flavors of this classic Southern dish!

Feel free to customize this recipe by adding shrimp, crabmeat, or other seafood along with the chicken and sausage for a seafood jambalaya. Adjust the Cajun seasoning to your preferred level of spiciness.

Texas BBQ Brisket

Ingredients:

- 1 whole beef brisket, trimmed (10-12 pounds)
- 1/4 cup yellow mustard
- 1/4 cup beef rub or BBQ seasoning (store-bought or homemade)
- Wood chips or chunks for smoking (hickory, oak, or mesquite)

For the Beef Rub:

- 1/4 cup paprika
- 2 tablespoons brown sugar
- 1 tablespoon kosher salt
- 1 tablespoon black pepper
- 1 tablespoon garlic powder
- 1 tablespoon onion powder
- 1 tablespoon chili powder
- 1 teaspoon cayenne pepper (optional, for extra heat)

Instructions:

1. Preheat your smoker or grill to 225°F (110°C) using indirect heat.
2. In a small bowl, mix together all the ingredients for the beef rub until well combined.
3. Trim any excess fat from the brisket, leaving about 1/4 inch of fat on the surface. Pat the brisket dry with paper towels.
4. Spread a thin layer of yellow mustard all over the brisket. This will help the rub adhere to the meat.
5. Sprinkle the beef rub evenly over the entire surface of the brisket, pressing it into the mustard to adhere.
6. Once your smoker or grill is at the desired temperature, place the brisket directly on the grate fat-side up.
7. Add wood chips or chunks to the smoker for added smoke flavor. Close the lid and smoke the brisket for about 1 hour per pound, or until the internal temperature reaches 195-205°F (90-95°C) and the meat is tender. This will take about 10-12 hours for a 10-12 pound brisket.
8. Avoid opening the smoker or grill too often to maintain a consistent temperature and smoke level.

9. Once the brisket reaches the desired internal temperature, remove it from the smoker and wrap it tightly in aluminum foil. Let it rest for at least 1 hour to allow the juices to redistribute.
10. After resting, carefully unwrap the brisket and slice it against the grain into thin slices.
11. Serve your Texas BBQ brisket hot with your favorite BBQ sauce, coleslaw, potato salad, and cornbread on the side.
12. Enjoy the smoky, tender, and flavorful goodness of your homemade Texas-style BBQ brisket!

Maryland Crab Cakes

Ingredients:

- 1 pound lump crabmeat, picked over for shells
- 1/3 cup mayonnaise
- 1 large egg, lightly beaten
- 1 tablespoon Dijon mustard
- 1 tablespoon Worcestershire sauce
- 1 tablespoon Old Bay seasoning
- 1/4 teaspoon salt
- 1/4 teaspoon black pepper
- 1/4 cup finely chopped fresh parsley
- 1/4 cup finely chopped green onions (white and green parts)
- 1 cup Panko breadcrumbs, divided
- 2 tablespoons unsalted butter
- 2 tablespoons olive oil
- Lemon wedges, for serving

Instructions:

1. In a large mixing bowl, combine the lump crabmeat, mayonnaise, lightly beaten egg, Dijon mustard, Worcestershire sauce, Old Bay seasoning, salt, black pepper, chopped parsley, chopped green onions, and 1/2 cup of Panko breadcrumbs. Gently fold everything together until well combined, being careful not to break up the crabmeat too much.
2. Divide the crab mixture into equal portions and shape them into round patties, about 3 inches in diameter and 1 inch thick. Place the remaining 1/2 cup of Panko breadcrumbs on a plate and coat each crab cake evenly with breadcrumbs, pressing lightly to adhere.
3. In a large skillet, heat the unsalted butter and olive oil over medium heat. Once the butter is melted and the skillet is hot, carefully add the crab cakes in batches, making sure not to overcrowd the skillet. Cook the crab cakes for about 4-5 minutes on each side, or until golden brown and crispy, and heated through.
4. Transfer the cooked crab cakes to a plate lined with paper towels to drain any excess oil. Repeat with the remaining crab cakes, adding more butter and olive oil to the skillet as needed.

5. Serve the Maryland crab cakes hot with lemon wedges on the side for squeezing over the top.
6. Enjoy your homemade Maryland crab cakes as a delicious appetizer or main dish, with their crispy exterior and flavorful, tender crabmeat inside!

Boston Clam Chowder

Ingredients:

- 4 slices bacon, diced
- 1 onion, diced
- 2 stalks celery, diced
- 2 cloves garlic, minced
- 3 cups peeled and diced potatoes
- 2 cups clam juice
- 2 cups water
- 2 (6.5 oz) cans minced clams, drained, juice reserved
- 1 bay leaf
- 1/2 teaspoon dried thyme
- 1/4 teaspoon dried oregano
- Salt and pepper, to taste
- 2 cups half-and-half
- 2 tablespoons all-purpose flour
- Chopped fresh parsley, for garnish
- Oyster crackers, for serving

Instructions:

1. In a large pot or Dutch oven, cook the diced bacon over medium heat until crisp. Remove the bacon from the pot using a slotted spoon and set aside, leaving the bacon fat in the pot.
2. Add the diced onion and celery to the pot with the bacon fat and cook until softened, about 5 minutes. Add the minced garlic and cook for an additional 1-2 minutes, until fragrant.
3. Stir in the diced potatoes, clam juice, water, reserved clam juice from the canned clams, bay leaf, dried thyme, dried oregano, salt, and pepper. Bring the mixture to a boil, then reduce the heat to low. Cover and simmer for about 15-20 minutes, or until the potatoes are tender.
4. In a small bowl, whisk together the half-and-half and all-purpose flour until smooth. Slowly pour the mixture into the pot, stirring constantly, to thicken the chowder.
5. Add the drained minced clams and cooked bacon back to the pot. Stir to combine and heat through for about 5 minutes.

6. Taste the chowder and adjust the seasoning with additional salt and pepper, if needed.
7. Remove the bay leaf from the chowder before serving.
8. Ladle the Boston clam chowder into bowls and garnish with chopped fresh parsley. Serve hot with oyster crackers on the side.
9. Enjoy your homemade Boston clam chowder, with its creamy texture, savory flavor, and tender chunks of clam and potatoes!

Philly Cheesesteak Sandwich

Ingredients:

- 1 pound ribeye steak, thinly sliced
- 2 tablespoons vegetable oil
- 1 large onion, thinly sliced
- 1 large green bell pepper, thinly sliced
- Salt and pepper, to taste
- 4 hoagie rolls, split lengthwise
- 8 slices provolone cheese

Instructions:

1. Heat a large skillet over medium-high heat. Add 1 tablespoon of vegetable oil to the skillet.
2. Add the thinly sliced ribeye steak to the skillet in an even layer. Season with salt and pepper to taste. Cook, stirring occasionally, until the steak is browned and cooked through, about 3-5 minutes. Remove the steak from the skillet and set aside.
3. In the same skillet, add the remaining tablespoon of vegetable oil. Add the thinly sliced onion and green bell pepper to the skillet. Cook, stirring occasionally, until the vegetables are softened and lightly caramelized, about 5-7 minutes. Season with salt and pepper to taste.
4. Return the cooked steak to the skillet with the onions and peppers. Toss everything together until well combined. Remove the skillet from the heat.
5. Preheat your oven's broiler.
6. Place the split hoagie rolls on a baking sheet, cut-side up. Divide the steak, onion, and pepper mixture evenly among the rolls, placing it on one side of each roll.
7. Top each sandwich with 2 slices of provolone cheese.
8. Place the baking sheet under the broiler and broil for 1-2 minutes, or until the cheese is melted and bubbly and the edges of the rolls are toasted.
9. Remove the Philly cheesesteak sandwiches from the oven and serve immediately.
10. Enjoy your homemade Philly cheesesteak sandwiches hot, with their tender steak, sautéed onions and peppers, and gooey melted provolone cheese, all piled high on a toasted hoagie roll!

Mississippi Mud Pie

Ingredients:

For the crust:

- 1 ½ cups chocolate cookie crumbs (from about 20 chocolate sandwich cookies)
- 6 tablespoons unsalted butter, melted

For the filling:

- 1 cup heavy cream
- 8 ounces semisweet chocolate, chopped
- 1 teaspoon vanilla extract
- 1 pint chocolate ice cream, softened

For the topping:

- 1 ½ cups heavy cream
- 2 tablespoons powdered sugar
- 1 teaspoon vanilla extract
- Chocolate shavings or cocoa powder for garnish (optional)

Instructions:

1. Prepare the Crust:
    - Preheat your oven to 350°F (175°C).
    - In a mixing bowl, combine the chocolate cookie crumbs and melted butter until well mixed.
    - Press the mixture evenly into the bottom and up the sides of a 9-inch pie dish.
    - Bake the crust for 10 minutes, then remove from the oven and let it cool completely.
2. Make the Filling:
    - In a small saucepan, heat the heavy cream over medium heat until it just starts to simmer.

- Remove from heat and add the chopped chocolate. Let it sit for a minute, then stir until the chocolate is completely melted and smooth.
- Stir in the vanilla extract until well combined.
- Spread the softened chocolate ice cream evenly over the cooled crust.
- Pour the chocolate ganache filling over the ice cream layer.
- Place the pie in the freezer and let it chill for at least 4 hours, or until firm.

3. Prepare the Topping:
    - In a mixing bowl, whip the heavy cream, powdered sugar, and vanilla extract until stiff peaks form.
    - Spread the whipped cream over the chilled pie.
4. Garnish and Serve:
    - If desired, garnish the pie with chocolate shavings or a dusting of cocoa powder.
    - Slice and serve the Mississippi Mud Pie chilled.
    - Enjoy the decadent layers of chocolatey goodness!

This Mississippi Mud Pie is sure to satisfy any chocolate lover's cravings with its creamy texture and rich flavor. It's perfect for special occasions or any time you're in the mood for a luxurious dessert.

New England Clam Bake

Ingredients:

- Fresh clams (such as littleneck or soft-shell clams)
- Lobsters (optional)
- Corn on the cob
- Potatoes
- Onions
- Sausages (such as linguica or chorizo)
- Mussels (optional)
- Butter
- Salt
- Old Bay seasoning or other seafood seasoning blend
- Water or beer (for steaming)

Instructions:

1. Preparation:
    - Soak the clams in cold water for about 30 minutes to purge any sand or grit. Scrub them gently with a brush under running water.
    - If using lobsters, rinse them under cold water and remove the rubber bands from their claws.
2. Layering the Ingredients:
    - In a large pot or outdoor cooker, layer the ingredients starting with the potatoes and onions at the bottom.
    - Add the sausages on top of the potatoes and onions.
    - Arrange the lobsters, if using, on top of the sausages.
    - Place the corn on the cob around the edges of the pot.
    - Add the clams and mussels on top of the other ingredients.
    - Season everything generously with salt and Old Bay seasoning.
3. Steaming:
    - Pour water or beer into the pot, enough to create steam but not so much that it covers the ingredients completely.
    - Cover the pot tightly with a lid.
4. Cooking:
    - Place the pot over high heat and bring the liquid to a boil.

    - Once boiling, reduce the heat to medium and let the ingredients steam for about 20-30 minutes, or until the clams and mussels have opened, the lobsters are cooked through, and the potatoes are tender.
5. Serving:
    - Carefully remove the lid and check that all the seafood is cooked.
    - Transfer the contents of the pot to a large serving platter or directly onto a table covered with newspapers or butcher paper.
    - Serve with melted butter on the side for dipping.
6. Enjoy:
    - Gather your friends and family around the table and enjoy the delicious feast together!

A New England Clam Bake is a delightful way to celebrate the flavors of the sea and the bounty of the New England coast. Adjust the ingredients and quantities according to your preferences and the size of your gathering.

Kansas City BBQ Ribs

Ingredients:

For the ribs:

- 2 racks of pork baby back ribs (about 4-5 pounds total)
- Kansas City-style BBQ rub (store-bought or homemade)
- Yellow mustard (optional, for binding the rub)
- Wood chips for smoking (hickory, apple, or cherry wood)

For the Kansas City-style BBQ sauce:

- 2 cups ketchup
- 1/2 cup apple cider vinegar
- 1/2 cup packed brown sugar
- 1/4 cup honey
- 1/4 cup molasses
- 2 tablespoons Worcestershire sauce
- 1 tablespoon mustard
- 1 tablespoon chili powder
- 1 teaspoon garlic powder
- 1 teaspoon onion powder
- Salt and black pepper to taste

Instructions:

1. Prepare the Ribs:
    - Remove the membrane from the back of the ribs. Use a butter knife to loosen the membrane at one end of the rack, then grab it with a paper towel and peel it off.
    - Pat the ribs dry with paper towels.
    - Optional: If desired, rub a thin layer of yellow mustard over the ribs to help the rub adhere.
2. Apply the BBQ Rub:
    - Generously coat both sides of the ribs with the Kansas City-style BBQ rub. Make sure to massage the rub into the meat, covering it evenly.

3. Prepare the Smoker:
    - Preheat your smoker to 225°F (107°C). Add wood chips to the smoker box or directly to the coals for smoke flavor. Hickory, apple, or cherry wood are traditional choices for Kansas City-style ribs.
4. Smoke the Ribs:
    - Place the ribs on the smoker grate, bone-side down.
    - Close the lid and smoke the ribs for 3-4 hours, maintaining a steady temperature and adding more wood chips as needed to maintain smoke production.
    - The ribs are ready when the meat has pulled back from the ends of the bones and is tender but not falling off the bone.
5. Make the BBQ Sauce:
    - In a saucepan, combine all the ingredients for the Kansas City-style BBQ sauce over medium heat.
    - Stir well to combine and bring the sauce to a simmer.
    - Reduce the heat to low and let the sauce simmer for 15-20 minutes, stirring occasionally, until it thickens slightly.
    - Remove the sauce from heat and set aside.
6. Glaze the Ribs:
    - Brush the smoked ribs with a generous coating of the prepared BBQ sauce on both sides during the last 30 minutes of cooking.
    - Continue to cook the ribs until the sauce caramelizes and forms a sticky glaze.
7. Serve:
    - Once the ribs are done, remove them from the smoker and let them rest for a few minutes.
    - Slice the ribs between the bones and serve with extra BBQ sauce on the side.

Enjoy these delicious Kansas City BBQ Ribs with your favorite sides like coleslaw, baked beans, or cornbread for a true barbecue feast!

Wisconsin Beer Brats

Ingredients:

- 6 to 8 fresh bratwurst sausages
- 1 large onion, thinly sliced
- 2 bottles (12 ounces each) of your favorite beer (such as a lager or ale)
- 2 tablespoons butter
- 2 cloves garlic, minced (optional)
- Mustard, sauerkraut, and buns for serving

Instructions:

1. Prepare the Brats:
   - Prick the bratwurst sausages with a fork several times on each side. This helps them absorb more flavor while cooking.
2. Preheat the Grill or Stovetop:
   - If using a grill, preheat it to medium heat. If cooking indoors, you can use a large skillet or grill pan over medium heat.
3. Cook the Brats:
   - In a large skillet or grill pan, melt the butter over medium heat.
   - Add the sliced onions and minced garlic (if using) to the skillet and cook until softened and translucent.
   - Place the bratwurst sausages in the skillet with the onions.
   - Pour the beer over the brats and onions, covering them completely.
   - Bring the beer to a simmer, then reduce the heat to low.
   - Let the brats simmer in the beer and onions for about 20-25 minutes, or until they are fully cooked through.
4. Grill (Optional):
   - If desired, you can finish the brats on the grill after simmering them in the beer. Preheat the grill to medium-high heat.
   - Remove the brats from the skillet and grill them for a few minutes on each side, until they develop grill marks and a slightly crispy exterior.
5. Serve:
   - Serve the beer brats on buns with the cooked onions.
   - Offer mustard, sauerkraut, or other condiments of your choice on the side.
   - Enjoy your Wisconsin Beer Brats with a cold beer and some classic side dishes!

This recipe captures the essence of Wisconsin beer brats, with the beer-infused onions adding flavor and moisture to the juicy sausages. It's a simple and delicious dish that's perfect for any casual gathering or barbecue.

Tex-Mex Enchiladas

Ingredients:

For the filling:

- 1 lb ground beef or turkey
- 1 small onion, diced
- 2 cloves garlic, minced
- 1 can (15 oz) black beans, drained and rinsed
- 1 can (4 oz) diced green chilies
- 1 cup corn kernels (fresh, frozen, or canned)
- 1 teaspoon ground cumin
- 1 teaspoon chili powder
- Salt and pepper to taste
- 1 cup shredded cheese (cheddar, Monterey Jack, or a blend)

For the sauce:

- 2 tablespoons vegetable oil
- 2 tablespoons all-purpose flour
- 2 tablespoons chili powder
- 1 teaspoon ground cumin
- 1 teaspoon garlic powder
- 1/2 teaspoon dried oregano
- 2 cups chicken or vegetable broth
- Salt to taste

For assembling:

- 8-10 large flour tortillas
- Additional shredded cheese for topping
- Chopped fresh cilantro, diced tomatoes, sliced jalapeños, sour cream, and avocado for garnish (optional)

Instructions:

1. Prepare the Filling:
    - In a large skillet, cook the ground beef or turkey over medium heat until browned and cooked through. Drain off any excess fat.
    - Add the diced onion and minced garlic to the skillet with the meat and cook for 2-3 minutes until the onion is softened.
    - Stir in the black beans, diced green chilies, corn kernels, ground cumin, chili powder, salt, and pepper. Cook for another 2-3 minutes to heat through. Remove from heat and let cool slightly.
    - Stir in the shredded cheese until melted and well combined.
2. Prepare the Sauce:
    - In a saucepan, heat the vegetable oil over medium heat.
    - Whisk in the flour, chili powder, ground cumin, garlic powder, and dried oregano to make a roux. Cook for 1-2 minutes until fragrant.
    - Gradually whisk in the chicken or vegetable broth, stirring constantly to prevent lumps from forming.
    - Continue cooking until the sauce thickens, about 5 minutes. Season with salt to taste.
3. Assemble the Enchiladas:
    - Preheat your oven to 375°F (190°C).
    - Spread a thin layer of the sauce in the bottom of a 9x13-inch baking dish.
    - Place a spoonful of the filling mixture in the center of each tortilla and roll it up tightly. Place seam-side down in the baking dish.
    - Pour the remaining sauce over the enchiladas, spreading it evenly to cover.
    - Sprinkle additional shredded cheese over the top of the sauce.
4. Bake the Enchiladas:
    - Cover the baking dish with aluminum foil and bake in the preheated oven for 20-25 minutes, or until the enchiladas are heated through and the cheese is melted and bubbly.
    - Remove the foil and bake for an additional 5 minutes to lightly brown the cheese on top.
5. Serve:
    - Garnish the Tex-Mex Enchiladas with chopped fresh cilantro, diced tomatoes, sliced jalapeños, sour cream, and avocado, if desired.
    - Serve hot and enjoy!

These Tex-Mex Enchiladas are a delicious and satisfying meal that's perfect for a weeknight dinner or entertaining guests. Feel free to customize the filling and toppings to suit your taste preferences.

Florida Key Lime Pie

Ingredients:

For the crust:

- 1 1/2 cups graham cracker crumbs
- 1/4 cup granulated sugar
- 6 tablespoons unsalted butter, melted

For the filling:

- 1 can (14 ounces) sweetened condensed milk
- 4 large egg yolks
- 1/2 cup Key lime juice (freshly squeezed is best, but bottled works too)

For the topping (optional):

- Whipped cream
- Lime zest or slices for garnish

Instructions:

1. Preheat your oven to 350°F (175°C).
2. In a medium bowl, mix together the graham cracker crumbs, sugar, and melted butter until well combined.
3. Press the crumb mixture firmly into the bottom and up the sides of a 9-inch pie dish to form the crust.
4. Bake the crust in the preheated oven for 8-10 minutes, or until lightly golden brown. Remove from the oven and let it cool slightly.
5. In a separate bowl, whisk together the sweetened condensed milk and egg yolks until smooth.
6. Gradually add the Key lime juice to the condensed milk mixture, whisking constantly until well combined and smooth.
7. Pour the lime filling into the cooled crust, spreading it out evenly.
8. Bake the pie in the preheated oven for 15-20 minutes, or until the edges are set but the center still jiggles slightly.
9. Remove the pie from the oven and let it cool to room temperature, then refrigerate for at least 2 hours (or overnight) until completely chilled and set.

10. Before serving, you can optionally top the pie with whipped cream and garnish with lime zest or slices.
11. Slice and serve chilled. Enjoy your delicious Florida Key Lime Pie!

Feel free to adjust the sweetness or tartness to your preference by tweaking the amount of sugar or lime juice in the filling.

Memphis BBQ Pulled Pork

Ingredients:

For the dry rub:

- 3 tablespoons paprika
- 2 tablespoons dark brown sugar
- 1 tablespoon garlic powder
- 1 tablespoon onion powder
- 1 tablespoon chili powder
- 1 tablespoon ground cumin
- 1 tablespoon black pepper
- 1 tablespoon salt
- 1 teaspoon cayenne pepper (adjust to taste for spiciness)
- 1 (5-6 pound) pork shoulder or Boston butt roast

For the mop sauce (optional):

- 1 cup apple cider vinegar
- 1 cup water
- 1 tablespoon dark brown sugar
- 1 tablespoon hot sauce
- 1 tablespoon Worcestershire sauce
- 1 tablespoon dry rub seasoning

For serving:

- Your favorite barbecue sauce
- Hamburger buns or sandwich rolls

Instructions:

1. In a small bowl, mix together all the ingredients for the dry rub until well combined.

2. Rub the dry rub mixture generously all over the pork shoulder, covering it evenly. Wrap the seasoned pork shoulder tightly in plastic wrap and refrigerate it for at least 4 hours, or preferably overnight, to allow the flavors to penetrate the meat.
3. Preheat your smoker or grill to 225°F (110°C), using your favorite wood chips or chunks for smoking (hickory or apple wood work well for pork).
4. If using a mop sauce, combine all the ingredients for the sauce in a small saucepan over medium heat. Bring the mixture to a simmer, then remove it from the heat and let it cool slightly.
5. Place the seasoned pork shoulder on the smoker or grill, fat side up, and cook it low and slow for about 1.5 to 2 hours per pound, or until the internal temperature reaches 195-205°F (90-96°C) and the meat is tender and easily pulls apart with a fork.
6. If using a mop sauce, baste the pork shoulder with the sauce every hour during cooking.
7. Once the pork shoulder is done, remove it from the smoker or grill and let it rest for about 30 minutes to allow the juices to redistribute.
8. Use two forks to shred the pork shoulder into bite-sized pieces, discarding any excess fat.
9. Serve the pulled pork on hamburger buns or sandwich rolls, topped with your favorite barbecue sauce. You can also serve additional barbecue sauce on the side for dipping.
10. Enjoy your delicious Memphis BBQ Pulled Pork sandwiches with coleslaw, pickles, or any other favorite accompaniments!

This recipe captures the essence of Memphis-style barbecue with its flavorful dry rub and tender, smoky pulled pork. Adjust the seasonings and spices to suit your taste preferences.

New Orleans Gumbo

Ingredients:

For the roux:

- 1/2 cup vegetable oil or bacon fat
- 1/2 cup all-purpose flour

For the gumbo:

- 1 large onion, diced
- 1 bell pepper, diced
- 2 celery stalks, diced
- 3 cloves garlic, minced
- 1 pound andouille sausage, sliced (or other smoked sausage)
- 1 pound chicken thighs, boneless and skinless, diced
- 6 cups chicken broth
- 1 can (14.5 ounces) diced tomatoes
- 1 cup okra, sliced (fresh or frozen)
- 2 bay leaves
- 1 teaspoon dried thyme
- 1 teaspoon dried oregano
- 1 teaspoon paprika
- 1/2 teaspoon cayenne pepper (adjust to taste)
- Salt and black pepper to taste
- Cooked white rice for serving
- Chopped green onions for garnish
- File powder (optional)

Instructions:

1. In a large, heavy-bottomed pot or Dutch oven, heat the vegetable oil or bacon fat over medium heat. Gradually whisk in the flour to create a roux. Cook the roux, stirring constantly, for about 20-30 minutes or until it reaches a dark caramel color. Be careful not to burn it.
2. Once the roux is darkened, add the diced onion, bell pepper, celery, and minced garlic to the pot. Cook, stirring frequently, for about 5-7 minutes or until the vegetables are softened.

3. Add the sliced andouille sausage to the pot and cook for an additional 5 minutes, allowing it to brown slightly.
4. Add the diced chicken thighs to the pot and cook until they are no longer pink on the outside, about 5 minutes.
5. Pour in the chicken broth and diced tomatoes (with their juices) into the pot, stirring to combine.
6. Add the sliced okra, bay leaves, dried thyme, dried oregano, paprika, and cayenne pepper to the pot. Season with salt and black pepper to taste.
7. Bring the gumbo to a simmer, then reduce the heat to low and let it simmer, uncovered, for about 1.5 to 2 hours, stirring occasionally, until the flavors have melded and the gumbo has thickened to your desired consistency.
8. Taste and adjust the seasoning as needed, adding more salt, pepper, or cayenne pepper for spice.
9. If using file powder, sprinkle a small amount over the gumbo and stir it in. Let the gumbo simmer for an additional 5 minutes.
10. Serve the New Orleans gumbo hot over cooked white rice, garnished with chopped green onions.
11. Enjoy your delicious and comforting bowl of New Orleans gumbo, filled with a medley of flavors and spices!

This recipe yields a hearty and authentic New Orleans gumbo, but feel free to customize it by adding shrimp, crab, or other seafood, or adjusting the spice level to your preference.

Colorado Green Chili

Ingredients:

- 2 pounds pork shoulder, trimmed of excess fat and cut into bite-sized pieces
- 2 tablespoons vegetable oil
- 1 large onion, diced
- 4 cloves garlic, minced
- 2 cans (4 ounces each) diced green chiles (such as Hatch chiles), or about 1 cup fresh roasted and diced green chiles
- 2 jalapeño peppers, diced (optional, for extra heat)
- 2 cups chicken broth or pork broth
- 2 medium tomatoes, diced
- 1 teaspoon ground cumin
- 1 teaspoon dried oregano
- 1/2 teaspoon smoked paprika
- Salt and black pepper to taste
- Chopped fresh cilantro for garnish
- Lime wedges for serving
- Tortillas or crusty bread for serving

Instructions:

1. In a large pot or Dutch oven, heat the vegetable oil over medium-high heat. Add the diced pork shoulder pieces in batches and brown them on all sides. Remove the browned pork from the pot and set aside.
2. In the same pot, add the diced onion and cook until softened, about 5 minutes. Add the minced garlic and cook for an additional 1-2 minutes, until fragrant.
3. Return the browned pork to the pot. Add the diced green chiles, diced jalapeño peppers (if using), chicken or pork broth, diced tomatoes, ground cumin, dried oregano, and smoked paprika. Stir to combine.
4. Bring the mixture to a simmer, then reduce the heat to low. Cover the pot and let the green chili simmer gently for about 2-3 hours, stirring occasionally, until the pork is tender and the flavors have melded together.
5. Taste the green chili and season with salt and black pepper to taste.
6. Serve the Colorado green chili hot, garnished with chopped fresh cilantro and lime wedges on the side. Serve with tortillas or crusty bread for dipping and soaking up the delicious sauce.

7. Enjoy your hearty and flavorful Colorado green chili!

This recipe can be customized based on personal preferences. You can adjust the amount of green chiles and jalapeños to control the level of spiciness, and you can add other ingredients like diced potatoes or beans if desired.

Texas Sheet Cake

Ingredients:

For the cake:

- 2 cups all-purpose flour
- 2 cups granulated sugar
- 1 teaspoon baking soda
- 1/2 teaspoon salt
- 1 cup unsalted butter
- 1 cup water
- 1/4 cup cocoa powder
- 2 large eggs, lightly beaten
- 1/2 cup sour cream
- 1 teaspoon vanilla extract

For the frosting:

- 1/2 cup unsalted butter
- 1/4 cup cocoa powder
- 1/3 cup whole milk or half-and-half
- 1 teaspoon vanilla extract
- 3 cups powdered sugar
- 1 cup chopped pecans or walnuts (optional)

Instructions:

1. Preheat your oven to 350°F (175°C). Grease and flour a 15x10x1-inch baking sheet (jelly roll pan) or line it with parchment paper.
2. In a large mixing bowl, whisk together the flour, sugar, baking soda, and salt until well combined.
3. In a medium saucepan, combine the butter, water, and cocoa powder. Bring the mixture to a boil over medium heat, stirring constantly. Once it reaches a boil, remove it from the heat and pour it over the dry ingredients in the mixing bowl. Stir until smooth.

4. Add the lightly beaten eggs, sour cream, and vanilla extract to the mixing bowl, and stir until the batter is well combined and smooth.
5. Pour the batter into the prepared baking sheet, spreading it out evenly.
6. Bake the cake in the preheated oven for 20-25 minutes, or until a toothpick inserted into the center comes out clean.
7. While the cake is baking, prepare the frosting. In a medium saucepan, combine the butter, cocoa powder, and milk. Bring the mixture to a boil over medium heat, stirring constantly. Once it reaches a boil, remove it from the heat and stir in the vanilla extract.
8. Gradually whisk in the powdered sugar until the frosting is smooth and reaches your desired consistency. If using nuts, stir in the chopped pecans or walnuts.
9. As soon as the cake comes out of the oven, pour the warm frosting over the hot cake, spreading it out evenly with a spatula.
10. Allow the cake to cool completely in the pan before slicing and serving.
11. Serve the Texas sheet cake slices on a platter and enjoy! This cake is delicious on its own or served with a scoop of vanilla ice cream or a dollop of whipped cream.
12. Store any leftovers in an airtight container at room temperature for up to 3 days.

This recipe yields a moist and decadent Texas sheet cake that's perfect for serving at gatherings or enjoying as a special treat.

Chicago Hot Dog

Ingredients:

- 6 all-beef hot dogs
- 6 poppy seed hot dog buns
- Yellow mustard
- Neon green relish
- Chopped white onions
- Tomato slices
- Pickle spears
- Sport peppers
- Celery salt

Instructions:

1. Heat a pot of water over medium heat until it comes to a gentle simmer. Add the hot dogs and cook for about 5 minutes, or until heated through.
2. While the hot dogs are cooking, prepare the buns. Place them on a baking sheet and warm them in the oven at 350°F (175°C) for a few minutes, or until slightly toasted.
3. Place each hot dog in a bun.
4. Squeeze a line of yellow mustard along one side of each hot dog.
5. Add a generous amount of neon green relish on top of the mustard.
6. Sprinkle chopped white onions over the relish.
7. Place a tomato slice on top of the onions.
8. Add a pickle spear on the opposite side of the hot dog from the mustard.
9. Place a sport pepper on top of the pickle spear.
10. Lightly sprinkle celery salt over the assembled hot dog.
11. Serve your Chicago-style hot dogs immediately, and enjoy the delicious combination of flavors and textures!

Chicago-style hot dogs are traditionally served with a side of fries or potato chips and a cold drink. They're perfect for summer cookouts, baseball games, or anytime you're craving a tasty and satisfying meal.

New York Cheesecake

Ingredients:

For the crust:

- 1 1/2 cups graham cracker crumbs
- 1/4 cup granulated sugar
- 1/2 cup unsalted butter, melted

For the filling:

- 4 packages (8 ounces each) cream cheese, softened
- 1 1/4 cups granulated sugar
- 4 large eggs
- 1 cup sour cream
- 1 tablespoon all-purpose flour
- 1 tablespoon vanilla extract
- 1/4 teaspoon salt

For the topping (optional):

- 1 cup sour cream
- 1/4 cup granulated sugar
- 1 teaspoon vanilla extract

Instructions:

1. Preheat your oven to 325°F (160°C). Grease a 9-inch springform pan with butter or non-stick cooking spray.
2. In a medium bowl, combine the graham cracker crumbs, granulated sugar, and melted butter until the mixture resembles wet sand.
3. Press the crumb mixture evenly onto the bottom of the prepared springform pan, using the back of a spoon or a flat-bottomed glass to compact it.
4. In a large mixing bowl, beat the softened cream cheese and granulated sugar together until smooth and creamy.
5. Add the eggs one at a time, beating well after each addition.

6. Mix in the sour cream, flour, vanilla extract, and salt until fully incorporated and the batter is smooth.
7. Pour the filling over the crust in the springform pan, spreading it out evenly.
8. Place the cheesecake in the preheated oven and bake for 45-55 minutes, or until the edges are set but the center is slightly jiggly.
9. While the cheesecake is baking, prepare the optional topping by mixing together the sour cream, granulated sugar, and vanilla extract in a small bowl.
10. After the initial baking time, remove the cheesecake from the oven and carefully spread the sour cream topping over the hot cheesecake.
11. Return the cheesecake to the oven and bake for an additional 5-7 minutes.
12. Turn off the oven and leave the cheesecake inside with the door closed for 1 hour to gradually cool.
13. Remove the cheesecake from the oven and run a knife around the edge of the pan to loosen the cheesecake from the sides.
14. Allow the cheesecake to cool completely at room temperature, then refrigerate it for at least 4 hours, or preferably overnight, to chill and set.
15. Once chilled and set, release the springform pan and transfer the cheesecake to a serving platter.
16. Slice and serve your delicious New York cheesecake plain or with your favorite toppings, such as fresh fruit or fruit compote.

Enjoy the creamy richness and classic flavor of this iconic dessert!

California Fish Tacos

Ingredients:

For the fish:

- 1 pound firm white fish fillets (such as cod, tilapia, or halibut)
- 1/4 cup all-purpose flour
- 1 teaspoon ground cumin
- 1 teaspoon chili powder
- 1/2 teaspoon garlic powder
- 1/2 teaspoon paprika
- Salt and black pepper to taste
- Vegetable oil for frying

For the slaw:

- 2 cups shredded cabbage or coleslaw mix
- 1/4 cup chopped fresh cilantro
- 2 tablespoons mayonnaise
- 1 tablespoon lime juice
- Salt and black pepper to taste

For assembly:

- 8 small corn or flour tortillas, warmed
- Sliced avocado
- Sliced jalapeños (optional)
- Lime wedges
- Salsa or hot sauce (optional)

Instructions:

1. Start by preparing the slaw. In a large bowl, combine the shredded cabbage or coleslaw mix with chopped cilantro, mayonnaise, lime juice, salt, and black pepper. Toss until well combined. Set aside.
2. Prepare the fish by cutting it into small, manageable pieces, about the size of fish sticks.
3. In a shallow dish, combine the all-purpose flour, ground cumin, chili powder, garlic powder, paprika, salt, and black pepper. Mix well.

4. Heat vegetable oil in a large skillet over medium-high heat.
5. Dredge the fish pieces in the flour mixture, shaking off any excess.
6. Carefully place the fish pieces in the hot oil and fry until golden brown and cooked through, about 3-4 minutes per side, depending on the thickness of the fish. Remove the cooked fish from the skillet and drain on paper towels to remove excess oil.
7. To assemble the tacos, place a generous spoonful of the slaw onto each warmed tortilla.
8. Top the slaw with a few pieces of the fried fish.
9. Add sliced avocado and jalapeños (if using) on top of the fish.
10. Squeeze fresh lime juice over the assembled tacos and serve immediately with additional lime wedges and salsa or hot sauce on the side.
11. Enjoy your delicious California fish tacos with their fresh and zesty flavors!

Feel free to customize these tacos with your favorite toppings or sauces, such as diced tomatoes, sliced radishes, or a drizzle of creamy chipotle sauce. Serve them alongside rice and beans for a complete meal, or enjoy them as a light and satisfying snack.

Maine Lobster Roll

Ingredients:

- 1 1/2 pounds cooked lobster meat, chopped into bite-sized pieces (about 4-5 lobster tails)
- 1/4 cup mayonnaise
- 2 tablespoons chopped fresh chives or green onions
- 1 tablespoon fresh lemon juice
- Salt and black pepper to taste
- 4 New England-style hot dog buns
- 2 tablespoons unsalted butter, melted
- Optional: Chopped fresh parsley for garnish, lemon wedges for serving

Instructions:

1. In a large mixing bowl, combine the chopped lobster meat, mayonnaise, chopped chives or green onions, and fresh lemon juice. Gently toss until the lobster meat is evenly coated with the mayo mixture. Season with salt and black pepper to taste. Set aside.
2. Heat a skillet or griddle over medium heat. Brush the inside of each New England-style hot dog bun with melted butter.
3. Place the buttered buns on the skillet or griddle, cut side down, and toast them until golden brown and lightly crispy, about 1-2 minutes per side. Remove from heat.
4. Divide the prepared lobster mixture evenly among the toasted buns, spooning it into each bun.
5. Garnish the lobster rolls with chopped fresh parsley, if desired.
6. Serve the Maine lobster rolls immediately, accompanied by lemon wedges on the side.

Enjoy the deliciousness of these classic Maine lobster rolls, filled with tender lobster meat and a creamy, flavorful dressing, all nestled in a buttery, toasted bun!

These lobster rolls are best served fresh and enjoyed right away. They make a perfect summer meal or a special treat for any occasion. Pair them with a side of coleslaw, potato chips, or a simple green salad for a complete and satisfying meal.

Hawaiian Huli Huli Chicken

Ingredients:

For the marinade:

- 1 cup pineapple juice
- 1/2 cup soy sauce
- 1/2 cup brown sugar
- 1/4 cup ketchup
- 1/4 cup rice vinegar
- 2 tablespoons sesame oil
- 2 tablespoons minced fresh ginger
- 2 cloves garlic, minced
- 1 teaspoon sriracha or chili garlic sauce (optional, for a spicy kick)
- Salt and black pepper to taste

For the chicken:

- 4 boneless, skinless chicken breasts or 8 bone-in chicken thighs
- Pineapple slices for garnish (optional)
- Chopped green onions for garnish (optional)
- Cooked rice for serving

Instructions:

1. In a mixing bowl, whisk together all the marinade ingredients until the sugar is dissolved and the marinade is well combined.
2. Place the chicken breasts or thighs in a large resealable plastic bag or a shallow dish. Pour the marinade over the chicken, making sure it is well coated. Seal the bag or cover the dish and marinate in the refrigerator for at least 2 hours, or preferably overnight, turning the chicken occasionally to ensure even marination.
3. Preheat your grill to medium-high heat (about 375-400°F or 190-200°C).
4. Remove the chicken from the marinade, shaking off any excess, and discard the remaining marinade.
5. Place the chicken on the preheated grill and cook for 6-8 minutes per side (for chicken breasts) or 8-10 minutes per side (for chicken thighs), or until the

chicken is cooked through and has nice grill marks. The internal temperature should reach 165°F (75°C).

6. While the chicken is grilling, you can brush it with any remaining marinade for extra flavor, but make sure to do so only during the last few minutes of cooking to avoid cross-contamination.
7. Once the chicken is cooked through, remove it from the grill and let it rest for a few minutes before slicing or serving.
8. Serve the Hawaiian Huli Huli Chicken hot, garnished with pineapple slices and chopped green onions if desired, and alongside cooked rice.

Enjoy the delicious flavors of Hawaiian Huli Huli Chicken, with its sweet and tangy marinade and tender, grilled chicken. It's perfect for a summer barbecue or any time you're craving a taste of the islands!

Southern Shrimp and Grits

Ingredients:

For the grits:

- 1 cup stone-ground grits
- 4 cups water or chicken broth
- 1 teaspoon salt
- 1/2 cup grated sharp cheddar cheese
- 2 tablespoons unsalted butter
- Salt and black pepper to taste

For the shrimp:

- 1 pound large shrimp, peeled and deveined
- 2 tablespoons Cajun seasoning (store-bought or homemade)
- 2 tablespoons unsalted butter
- 2 cloves garlic, minced
- 1 cup diced bell peppers (any color)
- 1/2 cup diced onion
- 1/2 cup diced celery
- 1 cup diced tomatoes (fresh or canned)
- 1/2 cup chicken broth or white wine
- 2 tablespoons chopped fresh parsley
- Salt and black pepper to taste
- Lemon wedges for serving

Instructions:

1. In a large saucepan, bring the water or chicken broth to a boil. Stir in the grits and salt. Reduce the heat to low and simmer, stirring occasionally, for about 20-25 minutes, or until the grits are thick and creamy.
2. Stir in the grated cheddar cheese and butter until melted and well combined. Season with salt and black pepper to taste. Cover and keep warm while preparing the shrimp.
3. Season the shrimp with Cajun seasoning, tossing to coat evenly.

4. In a large skillet, melt the butter over medium heat. Add the minced garlic and sauté for about 30 seconds, or until fragrant.
5. Add the diced bell peppers, onion, and celery to the skillet. Cook, stirring occasionally, for about 5 minutes, or until the vegetables are softened.
6. Add the seasoned shrimp to the skillet and cook for 2-3 minutes per side, or until they turn pink and opaque.
7. Stir in the diced tomatoes and chicken broth or white wine. Bring the mixture to a simmer and cook for another 2-3 minutes, allowing the flavors to meld together. Season with salt and black pepper to taste.
8. To serve, divide the creamy grits among serving bowls. Top with the shrimp and vegetable mixture, spooning the sauce over the top. Sprinkle with chopped fresh parsley and serve with lemon wedges on the side.
9. Enjoy your delicious Southern shrimp and grits as a comforting and satisfying meal!

This dish is perfect for brunch, lunch, or dinner, and it's sure to impress with its rich flavors and hearty texture. Feel free to customize the dish by adding other ingredients like bacon, sausage, or additional vegetables to suit your taste preferences.

Philadelphia Soft Pretzels

Ingredients:

For the dough:

- 1 1/2 cups warm water (110-115°F)
- 1 tablespoon granulated sugar
- 2 teaspoons active dry yeast
- 4 1/2 cups all-purpose flour
- 1 teaspoon salt

For boiling:

- 10 cups water
- 2/3 cup baking soda

For topping:

- Coarse salt or pretzel salt
- Melted butter for brushing (optional)

Instructions:

1. In a large mixing bowl, combine the warm water and sugar. Sprinkle the active dry yeast over the water and let it sit for about 5 minutes, or until foamy.
2. Add the flour and salt to the yeast mixture. Stir until a dough forms.
3. Turn the dough out onto a lightly floured surface and knead for about 5-7 minutes, or until the dough is smooth and elastic.
4. Place the dough in a greased bowl, cover with a clean kitchen towel or plastic wrap, and let it rise in a warm, draft-free place for about 1 hour, or until doubled in size.
5. Preheat your oven to 450°F (230°C). Line a baking sheet with parchment paper and lightly grease it.
6. Punch down the risen dough and divide it into 12 equal pieces. Roll each piece into a rope about 20 inches long.

7. To form the pretzels, shape each rope into a U-shape. Cross the ends over each other, then twist them around each other once. Bring the ends down to the bottom of the U-shape and press to form the classic pretzel shape. Place the shaped pretzels on the prepared baking sheet.
8. In a large pot, bring the 10 cups of water to a boil. Once boiling, add the baking soda and stir until dissolved.
9. Carefully lower the pretzels, one or two at a time, into the boiling water. Boil for about 30 seconds on each side, then remove them with a slotted spoon and place them back on the baking sheet.
10. Sprinkle the boiled pretzels with coarse salt while they are still wet.
11. Bake the pretzels in the preheated oven for 12-15 minutes, or until golden brown and cooked through.
12. Optional: Brush the baked pretzels with melted butter for extra flavor and shine.
13. Let the pretzels cool slightly before serving. Enjoy your homemade Philadelphia soft pretzels warm, with mustard or your favorite dipping sauce!

These homemade soft pretzels are best enjoyed fresh out of the oven, but you can store any leftovers in an airtight container at room temperature for up to 2 days. Reheat them in the oven for a few minutes before serving to restore their chewy texture.

Louisiana Crawfish Boil

Ingredients:

- 30-40 pounds live crawfish, rinsed and purged
- 5 gallons water
- 5 pounds small red potatoes
- 6 ears corn on the cob, shucked and halved
- 2 pounds smoked sausage (such as andouille), cut into 2-inch pieces
- 4 onions, peeled and quartered
- 4 lemons, halved
- 1/2 cup salt
- 1/2 cup Cajun or seafood boil seasoning
- 8 cloves garlic, peeled
- 6 bay leaves
- 2 tablespoons whole black peppercorns
- 1/4 cup hot sauce (optional)
- Additional seasoning to taste (such as Old Bay seasoning or cayenne pepper)

Instructions:

1. In a large stockpot or outdoor boiling pot, bring the water to a rolling boil.
2. Add the salt, Cajun seasoning, garlic, bay leaves, black peppercorns, and hot sauce (if using) to the boiling water. Stir to combine.
3. Add the quartered onions and halved lemons to the pot. Allow the mixture to return to a boil.
4. Once the water is boiling again, add the red potatoes to the pot. Cook for about 10 minutes.
5. Add the smoked sausage pieces to the pot and cook for an additional 5 minutes.
6. Add the corn on the cob halves to the pot and cook for another 5 minutes.
7. Finally, add the live crawfish to the pot. Stir well to ensure that all ingredients are submerged in the boiling water.
8. Bring the water back to a boil and then reduce the heat to medium-high. Let the crawfish boil for about 10-12 minutes.
9. Turn off the heat and let the crawfish soak in the hot water for an additional 15-20 minutes. This allows the crawfish to soak up the flavors of the seasoning.
10. After soaking, carefully drain the crawfish and other ingredients from the pot using a large colander or scoop basket.

11. Spread the boiled crawfish, potatoes, sausage, corn, onions, and lemons onto a large table covered with newspaper or butcher paper.
12. Serve the Louisiana crawfish boil hot, along with additional seasoning if desired, and provide plenty of napkins, melted butter, and dipping sauces like cocktail sauce or remoulade.

Enjoy the vibrant flavors and communal atmosphere of a traditional Louisiana crawfish boil with friends and family!

San Francisco Cioppino

Ingredients:

- 2 tablespoons olive oil
- 1 large onion, diced
- 4 cloves garlic, minced
- 1 green bell pepper, diced
- 1 red bell pepper, diced
- 1 fennel bulb, diced
- 1 teaspoon dried oregano
- 1 teaspoon dried basil
- 1/2 teaspoon crushed red pepper flakes (adjust to taste)
- Salt and black pepper to taste
- 1 cup dry white wine
- 1 can (28 ounces) crushed tomatoes
- 4 cups seafood broth or clam juice
- 1 bay leaf
- 1 pound large shrimp, peeled and deveined
- 1 pound firm white fish fillets (such as halibut or cod), cut into chunks
- 1 pound mussels, scrubbed and debearded
- 1 pound clams, scrubbed
- 1 pound crab legs or cooked crab meat
- Chopped fresh parsley for garnish
- Crusty bread for serving

Instructions:

1. In a large pot or Dutch oven, heat the olive oil over medium heat. Add the diced onion, minced garlic, diced bell peppers, and diced fennel. Cook, stirring occasionally, until the vegetables are softened, about 5-7 minutes.
2. Stir in the dried oregano, dried basil, crushed red pepper flakes, salt, and black pepper. Cook for another minute until fragrant.
3. Pour in the white wine and deglaze the pot, scraping up any browned bits from the bottom. Allow the wine to simmer for a few minutes until slightly reduced.
4. Add the crushed tomatoes, seafood broth or clam juice, and bay leaf to the pot. Stir to combine and bring the mixture to a simmer.
5. Reduce the heat to low and let the broth simmer, uncovered, for about 20-30 minutes to allow the flavors to meld together and the broth to slightly thicken.

6. Once the broth has simmered and developed flavor, add the shrimp, fish chunks, mussels, clams, and crab legs to the pot. Cover and simmer for about 5-7 minutes, or until the seafood is cooked through and the mussels and clams have opened.
7. Discard any mussels or clams that did not open during cooking.
8. Taste the cioppino and adjust the seasoning as needed with salt, pepper, or additional crushed red pepper flakes.
9. Ladle the San Francisco Cioppino into bowls, making sure to distribute the seafood and broth evenly. Garnish with chopped fresh parsley.
10. Serve the cioppino hot, accompanied by crusty bread for dipping into the flavorful broth.

Enjoy the rich and vibrant flavors of San Francisco Cioppino, a delicious seafood stew that's perfect for a special occasion or a cozy dinner at home!

Texas Chili Dogs

Ingredients:

For the chili:

- 1 tablespoon vegetable oil
- 1 onion, diced
- 2 cloves garlic, minced
- 1 pound ground beef
- 1 can (14.5 ounces) diced tomatoes
- 1 can (8 ounces) tomato sauce
- 1 can (15 ounces) kidney beans, drained and rinsed
- 2 tablespoons chili powder
- 1 teaspoon ground cumin
- 1 teaspoon paprika
- 1/2 teaspoon dried oregano
- Salt and black pepper to taste

For the hot dogs:

- 8 hot dog buns
- 8 beef hot dogs
- Desired toppings (such as shredded cheese, diced onions, pickled jalapeños, sour cream, etc.)

Instructions:

1. In a large skillet or Dutch oven, heat the vegetable oil over medium heat. Add the diced onion and minced garlic, and cook until softened, about 5 minutes.
2. Add the ground beef to the skillet and cook, breaking it up with a spoon, until browned and cooked through.
3. Stir in the diced tomatoes, tomato sauce, kidney beans, chili powder, ground cumin, paprika, dried oregano, salt, and black pepper.
4. Bring the chili mixture to a simmer, then reduce the heat to low. Let the chili simmer, uncovered, for about 20-30 minutes, stirring occasionally, until thickened and flavors have melded together. Adjust seasoning to taste.
5. While the chili is simmering, prepare the hot dogs. Grill or boil the hot dogs according to your preference until heated through.

6. Place each grilled or boiled hot dog in a bun.
7. Once the chili is ready, spoon a generous amount of chili over each hot dog.
8. Top the chili dogs with desired toppings such as shredded cheese, diced onions, pickled jalapeños, sour cream, etc.
9. Serve the Texas chili dogs hot and enjoy the delicious combination of spicy chili and juicy hot dogs!

These Texas chili dogs are perfect for a casual meal or for serving at a backyard barbecue. Customize them with your favorite toppings and enjoy the bold flavors of Texas chili in every bite!

Kentucky Hot Brown

Ingredients:

For the Mornay sauce:

- 2 tablespoons unsalted butter
- 2 tablespoons all-purpose flour
- 1 1/2 cups milk
- 1 cup shredded sharp cheddar cheese
- 1/4 cup grated Parmesan cheese
- Salt and black pepper to taste
- Pinch of nutmeg (optional)

For assembling:

- 4 thick slices of bread (such as Texas toast or sourdough)
- 8 slices cooked turkey breast
- 8 slices cooked bacon
- 2 ripe tomatoes, sliced
- Paprika for garnish
- Chopped fresh parsley for garnish

Instructions:

1. To make the Mornay sauce, melt the butter in a saucepan over medium heat. Add the flour and whisk continuously for about 1-2 minutes to make a roux.
2. Gradually whisk in the milk, stirring constantly to prevent lumps from forming. Cook until the mixture thickens and comes to a simmer.
3. Reduce the heat to low and stir in the shredded cheddar cheese and grated Parmesan cheese until melted and smooth. Season with salt, black pepper, and a pinch of nutmeg if desired. Remove from heat and set aside.
4. Preheat your broiler to high.
5. Place the slices of bread on a baking sheet and toast them under the broiler for a few minutes on each side until golden brown.
6. Remove the toasted bread from the oven and top each slice with 2 slices of cooked turkey breast.
7. Arrange 2 slices of cooked bacon on top of the turkey on each slice of bread.
8. Place 2 slices of tomato on top of the bacon on each slice of bread.

9. Spoon the prepared Mornay sauce over each open-faced sandwich, covering the turkey, bacon, and tomato.
10. Sprinkle paprika over the Mornay sauce for color.
11. Return the assembled sandwiches to the broiler and broil for 3-5 minutes, or until the sauce is bubbly and lightly golden brown.
12. Remove the Kentucky Hot Browns from the oven and garnish with chopped fresh parsley.
13. Serve the Kentucky Hot Browns hot and enjoy the rich and savory flavors!

These Kentucky Hot Browns make a delicious and satisfying meal, perfect for brunch, lunch, or a cozy dinner at home. Serve them alongside a crisp green salad or your favorite side dish for a complete and comforting meal.

Vermont Maple Syrup Pancakes

Ingredients:

- 1 1/2 cups all-purpose flour
- 2 tablespoons granulated sugar
- 1 tablespoon baking powder
- 1/2 teaspoon salt
- 1 1/4 cups milk
- 1 large egg
- 3 tablespoons unsalted butter, melted
- Pure Vermont maple syrup, for serving
- Butter, for serving (optional)

Instructions:

1. In a large mixing bowl, whisk together the flour, sugar, baking powder, and salt until well combined.
2. In a separate bowl, whisk together the milk and egg until smooth.
3. Pour the melted butter into the milk and egg mixture and whisk until well incorporated.
4. Pour the wet ingredients into the dry ingredients and stir until just combined. Be careful not to overmix; a few lumps in the batter are okay.
5. Heat a non-stick skillet or griddle over medium heat. Lightly grease the surface with butter or cooking spray.
6. Once the skillet or griddle is hot, pour about 1/4 cup of batter onto the surface for each pancake. Use the back of a spoon or a ladle to spread the batter into a round shape, if necessary.
7. Cook the pancakes for 2-3 minutes, or until bubbles form on the surface and the edges begin to look set.
8. Flip the pancakes with a spatula and cook for an additional 1-2 minutes, or until golden brown and cooked through.
9. Remove the pancakes from the skillet or griddle and keep warm.
10. Repeat the process with the remaining batter, greasing the skillet or griddle as needed.
11. Serve the Vermont maple syrup pancakes hot, drizzled with pure Vermont maple syrup and topped with a pat of butter, if desired.

12. Enjoy your delicious homemade pancakes with the rich, natural sweetness of pure Vermont maple syrup!

These Vermont maple syrup pancakes are perfect for a cozy weekend breakfast or brunch. Serve them with your favorite breakfast sides such as crispy bacon, fresh fruit, or scrambled eggs for a satisfying meal that everyone will love.

Tennessee Hot Chicken

Ingredients:

For the chicken:

- 4 bone-in, skin-on chicken thighs
- 4 bone-in, skin-on chicken drumsticks
- Salt and black pepper to taste
- 1 cup buttermilk
- 2 cups all-purpose flour
- Vegetable oil, for frying

For the hot sauce:

- 1/2 cup hot sauce (such as cayenne pepper sauce)
- 1/4 cup unsalted butter, melted
- 1 tablespoon brown sugar
- 1 teaspoon paprika
- 1/2 teaspoon garlic powder
- 1/2 teaspoon onion powder
- 1/2 teaspoon cayenne pepper (adjust to taste)
- Salt to taste

For serving:

- Sliced white bread or sandwich buns
- Pickles slices
- Coleslaw (optional)

Instructions:

1. Season the chicken thighs and drumsticks with salt and black pepper to taste.
2. Place the seasoned chicken pieces in a large bowl and pour the buttermilk over them, ensuring they are fully coated. Cover the bowl and refrigerate for at least 1 hour, or overnight for best results.
3. In a shallow dish or bowl, combine the all-purpose flour with additional salt and black pepper to taste.
4. Remove the chicken from the buttermilk, allowing any excess to drip off. Dredge each piece of chicken in the seasoned flour, shaking off any excess.

5. Heat vegetable oil in a large skillet or Dutch oven to 350°F (175°C) for frying.
6. Carefully add the coated chicken pieces to the hot oil, working in batches if necessary to avoid overcrowding the skillet. Fry the chicken for about 12-15 minutes, turning occasionally, until golden brown and cooked through. The internal temperature should reach 165°F (75°C).
7. While the chicken is frying, prepare the hot sauce. In a small bowl, whisk together the hot sauce, melted butter, brown sugar, paprika, garlic powder, onion powder, cayenne pepper, and salt until well combined. Adjust the seasoning and spiciness according to your preference.
8. Once the chicken is cooked, remove it from the oil and drain on a wire rack or paper towels.
9. Dip each piece of fried chicken into the hot sauce mixture, ensuring it is evenly coated with the spicy sauce.
10. Serve the Tennessee hot chicken immediately on sliced white bread or sandwich buns, topped with pickle slices and coleslaw if desired.
11. Enjoy the fiery and flavorful goodness of homemade Tennessee hot chicken!

This dish is perfect for spice lovers and makes a deliciously indulgent meal. Serve it with your favorite sides and enjoy the bold flavors of Nashville-style hot chicken right at home.

Detroit-Style Coney Dog

Ingredients:

For the chili:

- 1 tablespoon vegetable oil
- 1 small onion, finely chopped
- 2 cloves garlic, minced
- 1 pound ground beef
- 1 can (14.5 ounces) crushed tomatoes
- 1 tablespoon tomato paste
- 1 tablespoon chili powder
- 1 teaspoon ground cumin
- 1/2 teaspoon paprika
- 1/4 teaspoon cayenne pepper (optional, for extra heat)
- Salt and black pepper to taste

For assembling:

- 8 beef hot dogs
- 8 hot dog buns
- Yellow mustard
- Diced onions

Instructions:

1. In a large skillet or Dutch oven, heat the vegetable oil over medium heat. Add the chopped onion and minced garlic, and cook until softened, about 5 minutes.
2. Add the ground beef to the skillet and cook, breaking it up with a spoon, until browned and cooked through.
3. Stir in the crushed tomatoes, tomato paste, chili powder, ground cumin, paprika, cayenne pepper (if using), salt, and black pepper. Simmer the chili mixture for about 15-20 minutes, stirring occasionally, until thickened and flavorful. Adjust seasoning to taste.
4. While the chili is simmering, grill or boil the hot dogs according to your preference until heated through.
5. Steam the hot dog buns until warm and soft.

6. To assemble the Detroit-style Coney dogs, place a grilled hot dog in each steamed bun.
7. Spoon a generous amount of the chili over each hot dog.
8. Drizzle yellow mustard over the chili, followed by a sprinkle of diced onions.
9. Serve the Detroit-style Coney dogs immediately, with extra chili and toppings on the side if desired.
10. Enjoy the delicious combination of flavors and textures in these iconic Detroit-style Coney dogs!

These Coney dogs are perfect for a casual meal or for serving at a backyard barbecue. Customize them with your favorite toppings and enjoy the bold flavors of this Detroit classic right at home.

Hawaiian Loco Moco

Ingredients:

For the hamburger patties:

- 1 pound ground beef
- 1/4 cup breadcrumbs
- 1/4 cup chopped onion
- 1 clove garlic, minced
- 1 egg
- Salt and black pepper to taste
- Vegetable oil for frying

For the brown gravy:

- 2 tablespoons unsalted butter
- 2 tablespoons all-purpose flour
- 2 cups beef broth
- 2 tablespoons soy sauce
- Salt and black pepper to taste

For assembling:

- Cooked white rice
- Fried eggs (1 per serving)
- Sliced green onions for garnish (optional)
- Hot sauce (optional)

Instructions:

1. In a mixing bowl, combine the ground beef, breadcrumbs, chopped onion, minced garlic, egg, salt, and black pepper. Mix until well combined.
2. Divide the mixture into 4 equal portions and shape each portion into a hamburger patty.

3. Heat a skillet or griddle over medium heat and add a little vegetable oil. Cook the hamburger patties for about 4-5 minutes on each side, or until cooked through and browned. Remove from heat and set aside.
4. In the same skillet, melt the butter over medium heat. Stir in the flour to make a roux and cook, stirring constantly, for about 1-2 minutes.
5. Gradually whisk in the beef broth and soy sauce, stirring until the mixture is smooth. Bring to a simmer and cook for a few minutes, or until the gravy has thickened. Season with salt and black pepper to taste.
6. While the gravy is simmering, fry the eggs in a separate skillet or fry them according to your preference.
7. To assemble the Hawaiian Loco Moco, place a serving of cooked white rice on each plate.
8. Top the rice with a cooked hamburger patty.
9. Place a fried egg on top of each hamburger patty.
10. Spoon the brown gravy over the fried eggs and hamburgers.
11. Garnish with sliced green onions if desired, and serve hot.
12. Optional: Serve with hot sauce on the side for extra flavor.

Enjoy the deliciousness of Hawaiian Loco Moco, with its hearty combination of rice, hamburger patty, fried egg, and savory brown gravy. It's a satisfying and comforting dish that's perfect for breakfast, brunch, lunch, or dinner!

Texas Chicken Fried Steak

Ingredients:

For the steak:

- 4 beef cube steaks (about 4 ounces each), tenderized
- Salt and black pepper to taste
- 1 cup all-purpose flour
- 1 teaspoon garlic powder
- 1 teaspoon onion powder
- 1/2 teaspoon paprika
- 1/4 teaspoon cayenne pepper (optional)
- 2 large eggs
- 1/4 cup milk
- Vegetable oil, for frying

For the gravy:

- 2 tablespoons unsalted butter
- 2 tablespoons all-purpose flour
- 2 cups milk
- Salt and black pepper to taste

Instructions:

1. Season the cube steaks on both sides with salt and black pepper.
2. In a shallow dish, combine the all-purpose flour with garlic powder, onion powder, paprika, and cayenne pepper (if using). Mix well.
3. In another shallow dish, whisk together the eggs and milk until well combined.
4. Dredge each cube steak in the seasoned flour mixture, shaking off any excess.
5. Dip the floured cube steaks into the egg mixture, allowing any excess to drip off.
6. Dredge the steaks once again in the seasoned flour mixture, pressing gently to adhere the flour to the surface of the steaks.
7. Heat vegetable oil in a large skillet over medium-high heat until hot, but not smoking.

8. Carefully add the breaded cube steaks to the hot oil, working in batches if necessary to avoid overcrowding the skillet. Cook the steaks for 3-4 minutes per side, or until golden brown and crispy.
9. Once cooked, transfer the fried steaks to a wire rack or paper towels to drain excess oil.
10. To make the gravy, in a separate saucepan, melt the butter over medium heat. Stir in the flour to make a roux and cook, stirring constantly, for about 1-2 minutes.
11. Gradually whisk in the milk, stirring constantly to prevent lumps from forming. Cook the gravy, stirring occasionally, until it thickens and comes to a simmer.
12. Season the gravy with salt and black pepper to taste, adjusting the seasoning as needed.
13. Serve the Texas Chicken Fried Steak hot, topped with creamy gravy.
14. Enjoy your delicious homemade Texas Chicken Fried Steak with mashed potatoes, biscuits, or your favorite side dishes!

This dish is perfect for a hearty and satisfying meal, reminiscent of classic Southern comfort food.

California Club Sandwich

Ingredients:

- 8 slices of your favorite sandwich bread (such as whole wheat, sourdough, or multigrain)
- 8 slices cooked bacon
- 8 slices deli turkey breast
- 1 ripe avocado, sliced
- 1 large tomato, sliced
- 4 leaves of lettuce (such as green leaf or romaine)
- Mayonnaise, for spreading
- Salt and black pepper to taste
- Optional: sliced cheese (such as Swiss or cheddar)

Instructions:

1. Toast the slices of bread until golden brown and crispy.
2. Spread mayonnaise on one side of each slice of toast.
3. Layer the sandwich as follows: Start with a slice of toast (mayonnaise side up), then add a leaf of lettuce, followed by 2 slices of cooked bacon, 2 slices of deli turkey breast, a few slices of avocado, and a couple of slices of tomato. Season the tomato slices with salt and black pepper if desired.
4. If using cheese, add a slice on top of the tomato slices.
5. Top with another slice of toast (mayonnaise side down).
6. Repeat the layering process for the remaining sandwiches.
7. If desired, secure each sandwich with toothpicks and slice diagonally in half before serving.
8. Serve the California Club Sandwiches immediately, and enjoy them as a delicious lunch or light dinner option!

Feel free to customize your California Club Sandwich with additional ingredients like sliced red onion, sprouts, or your favorite condiments. These sandwiches are versatile and can be easily adjusted to suit your taste preferences.

New York Reuben Sandwich

Ingredients:

- 8 slices of rye bread
- 1 pound thinly sliced corned beef
- 1 cup sauerkraut, drained
- 8 slices Swiss cheese
- Russian dressing (store-bought or homemade)
- Butter or margarine, softened

Russian Dressing:

- 1/2 cup mayonnaise
- 2 tablespoons ketchup
- 1 tablespoon sweet pickle relish
- 1 teaspoon Worcestershire sauce
- 1/2 teaspoon garlic powder
- 1/2 teaspoon onion powder
- Salt and pepper to taste

Instructions:

1. If making Russian dressing, combine all dressing ingredients in a small bowl and mix well. Adjust seasoning to taste. Set aside.
2. Preheat a griddle or large skillet over medium heat.
3. Spread Russian dressing on one side of each slice of rye bread.
4. Layer corned beef, Swiss cheese, and sauerkraut on four of the bread slices (dressing side up).
5. Top each sandwich with the remaining bread slices (dressing side down), creating four sandwiches.
6. Spread softened butter or margarine on the outside of each sandwich.
7. Place sandwiches on the preheated griddle or skillet and cook for 3-4 minutes per side, or until the bread is golden brown and the cheese is melted.
8. Remove sandwiches from the griddle or skillet and let them cool for a minute before slicing in half.
9. Serve the New York Reuben sandwiches hot, with a side of coleslaw, pickles, or potato chips.

Enjoy the classic combination of flavors in this iconic New York deli sandwich, perfect for lunch or dinner!

Maryland Crab Soup

Ingredients:

- 1 pound lump crab meat, picked over for shells
- 4 cups seafood or chicken broth
- 1 can (14.5 ounces) diced tomatoes, undrained
- 1 cup frozen or canned corn kernels
- 1 cup frozen or canned lima beans
- 1 cup diced potatoes
- 1 cup diced carrots
- 1 cup diced celery
- 1 onion, diced
- 2 cloves garlic, minced
- 2 tablespoons vegetable oil
- 2 bay leaves
- 1 teaspoon Old Bay seasoning (or more to taste)
- Salt and black pepper to taste
- Chopped fresh parsley for garnish (optional)

Instructions:

1. In a large pot or Dutch oven, heat the vegetable oil over medium heat. Add the diced onion, minced garlic, diced celery, diced carrots, and diced potatoes. Cook, stirring occasionally, for about 5-7 minutes, or until the vegetables are softened.
2. Add the diced tomatoes (with their juices) to the pot, along with the seafood or chicken broth. Stir to combine.
3. Add the bay leaves and Old Bay seasoning to the pot, stirring to incorporate the seasoning.
4. Bring the soup to a simmer and cook for about 15-20 minutes, or until the vegetables are tender.
5. Add the frozen or canned corn kernels and lima beans to the pot. Simmer for an additional 5 minutes.
6. Gently fold in the lump crab meat, being careful not to break up the crab too much. Cook for another 5 minutes to heat through.
7. Season the soup with salt and black pepper to taste, and adjust the Old Bay seasoning if desired.
8. Remove the bay leaves from the soup before serving.

9. Ladle the Maryland Crab Soup into bowls and garnish with chopped fresh parsley if desired.
10. Serve the soup hot, accompanied by crusty bread or oyster crackers.

Enjoy the delicious flavors of Maryland Crab Soup, a comforting and hearty dish that's perfect for any occasion!

Chicago Italian Beef Sandwich

Ingredients:

For the Italian beef:

- 3 pounds beef sirloin or bottom round roast, trimmed of excess fat
- 4 cups beef broth
- 1 cup water
- 1 tablespoon Italian seasoning
- 1 tablespoon dried oregano
- 1 tablespoon dried basil
- 1 tablespoon garlic powder
- 1 teaspoon onion powder
- 1 teaspoon black pepper
- Salt to taste
- 4-6 Italian rolls or hoagie buns

For serving:

- Giardiniera (Italian pickled vegetables), for topping
- Sweet or hot peppers, sliced
- Provolone cheese slices (optional)

Instructions:

1. In a large pot or Dutch oven, combine the beef broth, water, Italian seasoning, dried oregano, dried basil, garlic powder, onion powder, black pepper, and salt. Bring the mixture to a simmer over medium heat.
2. Add the beef roast to the pot and simmer, covered, for 2-3 hours, or until the beef is tender and cooked through. Remove the beef from the pot and let it rest for a few minutes before slicing.
3. While the beef is resting, strain the broth to remove any solids and reserve it for dipping.
4. Slice the cooked beef thinly against the grain. You can use a sharp knife or a meat slicer for this step.

5. Preheat your oven broiler. Split the Italian rolls or hoagie buns and place them on a baking sheet, cut side up.
6. Arrange the sliced beef on the bottom half of each roll. Top the beef with a spoonful of the reserved broth.
7. If desired, add slices of provolone cheese on top of the beef.
8. Place the baking sheet under the broiler for 1-2 minutes, or until the cheese is melted and the bread is toasted.
9. Remove the baking sheet from the oven and assemble the sandwiches. Top the beef with giardiniera and sliced peppers.
10. Serve the Chicago Italian Beef Sandwiches hot, with additional broth for dipping on the side.

Enjoy the bold flavors of this iconic Chicago sandwich, perfect for lunch, dinner, or your next game day gathering!

Florida Key Lime Pie

Ingredients:

For the crust:

- 1 1/2 cups graham cracker crumbs
- 1/4 cup granulated sugar
- 6 tablespoons unsalted butter, melted

For the filling:

- 1 can (14 ounces) sweetened condensed milk
- 4 large egg yolks
- 1/2 cup key lime juice (freshly squeezed if possible)
- Zest of 1 lime (optional)

For the topping (optional):

- Whipped cream
- Lime slices or zest for garnish

Instructions:

1. Preheat your oven to 350°F (175°C).
2. In a mixing bowl, combine the graham cracker crumbs, granulated sugar, and melted butter. Stir until the mixture resembles coarse sand and holds together when pressed with your fingers.
3. Press the crumb mixture into the bottom and up the sides of a 9-inch pie dish, forming an even crust.
4. Bake the crust in the preheated oven for 8-10 minutes, or until lightly golden brown. Remove from the oven and let it cool while you prepare the filling.
5. In another mixing bowl, whisk together the sweetened condensed milk, egg yolks, key lime juice, and lime zest (if using) until smooth and well combined.
6. Pour the filling into the cooled graham cracker crust, spreading it out evenly.
7. Bake the pie in the preheated oven for 15-20 minutes, or until the filling is set but still slightly jiggly in the center.

8. Remove the pie from the oven and let it cool to room temperature, then refrigerate for at least 2 hours or until chilled and set.
9. Once chilled, top the pie with whipped cream and garnish with lime slices or zest if desired.
10. Slice and serve the Florida Key Lime Pie cold, and enjoy the refreshing and tangy flavors!

This classic dessert is perfect for any occasion, from casual gatherings to special celebrations. It's a taste of the tropics that's sure to please everyone's palate.

Milton Keynes UK
Ingram Content Group UK Ltd.
UKHW051917310524
443038UK00004B/18

9 798869 350572